COLD WAR PIANO

a volume of poems

COLD WAR PIANO

Doug May

Ober-Limbo Verlag

Acknowledgments

Thanks to the editors of *The Raw Art Review* ("The Yearning: I and II"), and *Rat's Ass Review* ("Loss Of Memory" and "North Of Flagstaff") for publishing my work. An earlier version of "Pandora's Inbox" appeared in *Aleola Journal of Poetry and Art.*

I am as always indebted to Karen Bowden for her invaluable encouragement and editorial advice. And to Henry Stanton for recognizing merit in the scribblings of an outsider.

Thanks to Laurie Holden for sharing his boyhood in Maine and for his support of the arts, all the arts. And to Henry Edelstein for being a good friend and keeping the champagne on ice until our herd achieves immunity.

Published by Ober-Limbo Verlag
Heidelberg, Germany

ISBN: 978-87-971569-6-4

Cover design and layout by Birgit Stephenson

For Greg and Birgit

(and for Kay Johnson of The Beat Hotel….
wherever she is)

CONTENTS

In Europe

Sometimes late in the afternoon
she will ask me a question like
“what was the name of the town
where we looked for porcelain?
You know, at the little shop
down the street from the market
where we bought the dirty bananas?”

And I will answer “Cordoba”
uncertainly, trying to squeeze
the sphinx-brown mosque
into a still life of porcelain
and dirty bananas.

“No, that was later,” she’ll reply.
“At this place the sheets smelled
like cedar planks and a peacock
flew in front of our window.”

“Charlottenlund?” I mumble,
staring at a budding
siren in an Elvira outfit
floating down the street,
her black gauze angles
whispering veiled threats.

“No,” she says. “Pay attention.
That was after Brussels...
don’t you remember
the beef stew and noodles
the blue Delft plates?”

It could be any of the
blank canvases I filled
with angels and devils
borrowed like ties
at the fancy restaurants
where I didn't belong.

The name doesn't matter
because she has already
left behind the lost city of
porcelain and dirty bananas
to wander other locales
short-lived as the blush
of tender grapes,
her mind crammed with
postcards of lobbies
and hot dog stands.

And as I listen to her
on this warm afternoon,
I envy how she remembers
a Europe I never noticed
and wonder what was
so urgent about finding
Vermeer's housemaid
reading a letter

or Holofernes
slain a dozen times
in a dozen different
municipal museums.

And I see the courtyard
where two old women
sat at an open window,
their faces creasing warily
into smiles.

They could have been
widows from Scranton
Denver or Topeka
gossiping at nightfall
and sharing the secrets
only women know.

Yet at that moment
they were Amsterdam itself.
So when I think of the city of
Spinoza and Rembrandt,
I touch the common hidden
things which run through
our fingers like water.

And when she asks me
"where did we stop to
admire the flowers
beside the dirty canal?"

I see centuries of heroines
and headless generals
swallowed up by
pouting tulips

the ancient occupants
of a neighborhood
elusive as a sigh.

1984—2021

Cold War Piano

I. Richter in America

At the Steinway a riveter with orange hair
communes with ghosts in the streets of
  Esterhazy Vienna.

The ancient school auditorium overflows,
lumbering motors recycle gossip
  and the rustle of programs

through Poupon-yellow graveyards of
bond rallies and school assemblies.
  The school nurse, beside my mother,

doesn't have her white compression
stockings on today.
  She is disappointed because

the program doesn't include
the Military Polonaise —
  "Beethoven iss so schwer," she says

with a disapproving frown.
It's the same look she makes
  when lecturing about the latest disease

or shaming a boy who smells like burnt
cheese. In the first row of seats
  the women of the guild

jab their snoring husbands, their towering
bouffants glowing like silver
  dandelions in the glare of a

Sonoran sunset. Near the city of Perm
a long allegro is interrupted
  by a work party of political prisoners

dumping a body into a pit and
covering it with lye.
  A captain lights a cigarette and

watches something in the distance,
dreaming of the mother who
  lies beneath their hoes

bursting into flowers in the spring.
Richter rises, the school nurse and
  my mother smile; in moments the aisle

will fill with bodies and the
intermission will begin. The prisoners
  rest on their hoes

glancing into the distance where
the same scene repeats itself
  every afternoon.

II. Cultural Exchange

After he shaved and got dressed,
the great pianist pretended to be
writing a letter or shining his
shoes. And when he peeked
through the transom and saw
an empty corridor, he crept
slyly down the red-carpeted
hallway toward freedom —
leaving the people's attaché

combing his walrus mustache
in a steamy bathroom mirror.

Strolling past auto showrooms
and drunks sprawled on
jail blankets, he thought to
himself how similar to Russia
was this mechanized flatness
serenaded by gaunt purple oxen.

The search party found him
an hour later, window shopping
at the downtown Woolworth's,
and urged the great Richter
nervously as lab techs
cradling a secret isotope
back to his red-carpeted
VIP suite at the Westward Ho.

After five Beethoven sonatas
and three Chopin etudes,
Richter waited behind the
suspicious eyes of his handlers
and autographed our programs —

square-jawed balding and
self-conscious as a schoolgirl
posing with fidgety beaus
straightjacketed into blazers
and polished wingtips.

None of them understood
the tragedy of what they'd heard:
the artist who owned nothing
but the encores he withheld

his love a secret mission
beneath fairground displays
of strutting Kalashnikovs
and swooping MIGs.

III. Elegy For A Music Teacher

Long ago you burst a vein
puttering in your garden,
just weeks removed from
the final day of class

the autumn sun of reflection
shriveling to a black iris
and mud-caked trowel
slipping from your grasp.

I remember your dry-cleaned
Brahmsian blazer and
how you'd navigate
the short flight of steps
to the studio with its

tubby Baldwin grands and
lyre-backed chairs. You
believed in the trembling silence
between each note
of a phrase

(nothing else mattered, not what
the politicians made of our confusion
not where we journeyed
after winter rolled like applause
from our hands).

These days no mushroom clouds
haunt whitewashed columns and
webby facades of the old
music building remodeled into

a spotless museum for Zuni pots
and dead-pawn Navajo blankets
spared the lots of burial grounds
bulldozed for condominiums —

I dig beneath plaster and drywall
to gather jumbled bones of
scales and arpeggios,
a vanished mezzo-soprano

still quarrels in the musty
air conditioning ducts
with air-raid signals
and scrambled jets

the Met's Saturday Tosca
slashed by an air-raid siren
warning us of monsters
too familiar to believe in.

(Sometimes I hear you
arguing with Beethoven —
what are all those arias
and fugues trying to say?

And Richter's there too,
rehearsing the Wanderer Fantasy
and smiling at the bad boys
smoking in the balcony....)

Desert Boy Suite

I. Prelude

Arise from shallow desert graves, you scenes
Of Piggly Wigglies, bustling hobby shops
And mobsters' castles flanked by putting greens —
Where old convention halls and tourist stops
In faded leisurewear collide with fleets
Of memory-effacing lightrail cars
And buttressed palo verdes and mesquites
Block out the sun of vanished cowboy bars.

II. Plaster City

Somewhere west of El Centro
my mind starts to wander
from the jungles of The Lost World
and cockpit of the Batmobile and
to pass the time I start counting
the sticky yellow galaxies
of millers and grasshoppers
clinging like bits of spinach omelet
to the windshield's iron skillet.
Up ahead, something is floating
in the afternoon light like a sullen
cloud indistinguishable from the
larger cloud that surrounds it
protectively. And as we get closer,
I begin to notice a few trees
and buildings set back from the road
in the haze of gypsum that
turns the sun into a flat orange disc
and bleaches the two-lane highway
the color of an adobe jailhouse.

My father rolls up the windows
and slows to a crawl. Leering
out of the middle distance,
the long blue skull of a T-rex
stands guard over a box
of tinker toys.

"What is it?" I ask him.
"Plaster City," he says.
"But if it's a city, where are the people?"
"Maybe it's their day off," he yawns
and shakes out a Newport
from the pack on the dash.

I can't believe there's a place
named after the stuff
they use to fill up holes,
a place that isn't even
a real place

just a cut in the earth
with no schools or churches
pretending to be
band aids.

Later I learned about miners
carving up the desert
for spare bedrooms
and kitchenettes
in tarantula suburbs
of shrinking horizons.

But on that day
the only thing I felt
was the weight of

dirty brown snow
and Christmas trees
dumped like soldiers
behind enemy lines.

III. One Street Over

was where the strangers lived. They had
the scorpions, we had the cucarachas.
Their children looked like grownups,
we were younger and still in love with
Duncan Renaldo and Howdy Doody.
Sometimes we pretended to be them
going door to door in dry-pressed blazers
peddling World's Finest Almond Bars
to raise money for the JV band.

Everyone in the world was Republican
but they were more Republican. They
raked and bagged their dry brown leaves
by noon, and still had the time to
remember the tiniest slight, whose
sister married a Jew or whose
babysitter stayed out all night.

We never played one street over.
The tamaracks were too old and dark
and smelled musty as reference books.
Somebody could have gotten lost
until he woke up on Saturday morning
bending over a water pump
with Les Elgart or Patti Page
on the Monkey Wards Zenith

grinning whiter than popping flashbulbs
and pre-sliced Wonder Bread.

IV. The Ape Man

He was a gift passed down by older kids
Like souvenirs of war, a mystery
Joe Hardy couldn't crack or Nancy Drew
Outsmart. The faceless drifter banished from
Our Dick and Janes, no one had seen him whizz
Upon a campfire ring or club and skin
A rabbit or a ringtail cat beneath
Unlucky stars. But from the wrinkled skins
Of spuds in campfire ash or zigzag lines
Carved into stumps I knew he'd passed that way
And left sure evidence of darker horrors —
A black sheep relative whose name
My mother hushed up like my IQ scores
When she ran out of Democrats to blame.

V. After The Conference

bits of runny egg
clung to my teeth

a song played on the
radio and the dog snored

in the sun. She gave me
a worried look

like she always did
when I'd told a fib

and I could hear my skin
squeak like an altar boy's

shoes during Easter service.
Suddenly I wasn't me

but a picture in a book
of freaks and miracles

with a long black bar
over my eyes

and a bunch of tiny words
that said stop, wait

look at this thing
what does it mean

is it the odd one out
or just another empty box?

VI. Storm Candles

They told me
I wasn't good enough
to join their club
because I got lost
with level 1 knots

and it took me forever
(plus a trip to the
emergency room)

to learn how to
ride a boy's bike.

After school they
liked to make fun of
my hand me down
angora jacket and
surplus sneakers

once they even
pinned me under
a sweaty dog pile and
rubbed my face in a
dead gopher.

But the one who didn't
laugh said that if
I agreed to meet him
in secret
he'd show me some
dirty pictures.

And one summer day
we went to the
white chapel of
Bermuda seed and
pools of 10W30

and he said to
lean my back against
the door
and keep quiet

while he pulled on
my weenie
like a farmer
milking a goat.

I didn't think any thing
in life could be
that easy, just

letting go and giving in
to the tilt of a
curious head and close
inviting smell of skin

sweet as yellow
Play-Doh
or Topps
bubblegum.

I thought he was my
forever friend

but one day he got tired
of fooling around
and started rumors
about me

after I leaned too close
angling for water
and light.

A few years ago
I saw him
pushing a cart

down the cabbage
and grapefruit aisle —

a lawyer or
senior accountant
with a bottle of Jim Beam
and a tired wife.

He probably had a
cabin in the woods
a mistress in silks
and a fancy ride

and I was just a mirage
burning storm candles —
not braving the lightning,
not sheltered inside.

VII. Playground

She was blonde and
talked like a grownup and
wore a plaid jumper
and Thom McCann shoes

and when she smiled at me
I got weak as sunflower tea
and started to shiver
like a deer that sniffs danger.

I carried her books home
a few times, and we sat on
the cloverleaf and she talked

(I could hear her words
leave little push marks
in the silence)

then out of nowhere
her face got hard
and worried

like she'd just remembered
something about me
she didn't want to know.

Afterwards another boy
carried her books home
and she still smiled

but in a way
that made me feel
like a gimp on crutches
accepting an award.

And from this I discovered
I would never be ready
for fate knocking with a
grown-up voice and
ice blue eyes

as long as younger kids
felt more my size.

VIII. Quiet Man

Not even grownups
knew the janitor who
haunted the church
grounds, sometimes he went
away and wildcatted or
fought fires in the dry pines
when he needed money
to buy whiskey
or play the horses.

He had one of those faces that
didn't stand out. But when I
spied on him from the
hedge outside his window

I heard two voices, one
smooth as egg nog pudding
and the other twisted and sharp
as a barbed wire fence.

Maybe he'd been doing it for years
carrying on an argument
with someone or something that
weighed on him
like a bushel of dead snakes.

Nobody knew which voice
belonged to him, the used car
salesman's
or the love sick tomcat's

and nobody
was going to ask.

IX. Rodeo Parade

In the old days we got to dress
like cowboys and cowgirls
and sit out in the sun to have
our pictures taken.
Class let out at noon so
everyone could head toward
Central Avenue hauling
lawn chairs and coolers,

turnstiles of sharp elbows
shoving us past
cotton candy barber poles
toward the curb where

Chamber of Commerce girls
or Job's Daughters
marched to the strains of
Washington Post and
La Paloma

their Annie Oakley hats
bobbing on root beer geysers
of ponytails.

I remember last of all
the Mormon elders
waving from a Conestoga wagon
feathered with
Comanche arrows

and high-stepping majorettes
of the Coyote marching band

with their fluoride smiles
and donut peach skins.

Two years from Ike's
Cubano mess but Dulles
still a hero to cowboys, housewives
and the UAW

America still One Nation
Under God

X. Report Card

While frowning at my C's and D's, she sighed.
Of course each individual was different
But there was always room for one who tried,
Outworked the slackers in the Ten Percent
And never let his rent or taxes slide.

She said I shouldn't strive for medicine
Or law, not everyone was made by God
The same so some must lean on next-of-kin
More than a gifted brain. And if my odds

Of getting rich and finding wedded bliss
Weren't great–why run a leaky boat aground?
The same forgetful sun would rise next day
Upon determined wannabe's unbound
By accidents of Sculptor's knife and clay.

She said a lot of complicated things
While sewing parachutes of apron strings.

Noir (An Ocean Of Red Herrings)

With apologies to Steve Hodel, John
Gilmore, James Ellroy and The Black Dahlia Solution

I. Femme Fatale

She was an innocent bride
of sunlight who rolled sailors
in Encino on Labor Day weekends.

Of middling height, always
wearing black except when
draped in blue, taupe or gray.

A faultless Helen
with rotting teeth
plugged with paraffin who

suffered the ravages
of intact hymen
and rampant nymphomania,

toiling under kliegs
of mustachioed directors
in abandoned warehouses

where she was never ID'd
by the LAPD
or the beat reporters.

The most unknown
in a century of unknowns
gassed in trenches
or cancelled in the womb.

And because of this
the fading picture
on a post office wall

or APB distant as
a leviathan wisp
of fedora-gray fog

never unmasked
never forgotten.

II. Extras

"In a movie, only the extras are real."
— Veronica Lake

That's all we were, just bit part extras
Roped off from the stars while cameras
Enshrined the next cleft chin or corn-fed girl
In rooms with outer views — the sly curl
Of a famous lip suggesting things
Best left unsaid, while loud insistent rings
From nightstand telephones or doorbell chimes
Forecast the slice and dice of filmic crimes.

Not Heroes, Cads or Girls Next Door,
We never had to learn fresh lines
Or prance through martinet's designs
With rouged eyes, elevated tits,
The frozen smiles of hypocrites.
But when the film went in the can,
Trudged home to lives without a plan.
To heartaches, mortgages and loss,
Our great lines buried in the dross
Of courtesy and cowardice.

We never knew why they chose us
Fresh off the midnight Greyhound Bus
To play stout Roman garrisons
Or Hitler's brash goose-stepping Huns.
Perhaps the way we smiled or stood
Revealed that in our candid blood
We knew *we'd* never take the hill,
Win fifty grand, or taste the thrill
Of clutching to our throats at last
A script girl's eager blonde repast:
Compliant, suave, yet full of spunk,
The conquest of the next dumb hunk
Costumed in spurs and cowboy hat
Or mobster's vest and snub-nosed gat.

III. Hollywood 1947

Velvet gloves of early evening pose
Upon a silver tray, a peacock strolls
Beside the goldleaf foils of melted sweets
And trampled black corsages. Olive Street
Has seen the worst, but nothing like the dark
And wormy rot she's pulled toward

In mincing steps. Despairingly toward
Another conga line another pose,
Pretending to be captured by the dark
Asides and whispered jokes on evening strolls
Down Sunset Boulevard or Franklin Street
Entangled with a sailor's "hons" or "sweets"

And boxes of adulterated sweets —
Too late for fate to bend, or luck to ward
Off prurient eyes drawn to the street
Of one-hour flops where gossip queens expose
Small-time producers' predatory strolls
With bottle blondes emerging from the dark.

What does he scheme, the cipher fueled by dark
Refusals, offering alluring sweets
And jaunts to Malibu? He's eyed her strolls
With officers and salesmen chumps toward
The prize withheld from him, watched them repose
Her torso, fueled by rage. The well-lit street

Where he grew up was nicknamed Easy Street
By those who toiled for dimes, yet he found dark
And darker ways to secretly oppose
His gilded fate in bare unfurnished suites,
Tattooing a velvet cake with leering strolls
Of Pall-Mall ash, bisecting it toward

The shank of 2 AM. The view toward
Hard curbs and vacant lots from Degnan Street
Lies crowned by throngs of stars on drunken strolls:
Brutish Orion with his flaming dark
Grimace pursues the Pleiades' charred sweets
Above a Dada mannequin's stiff pose.

Hearst ran the street, the cops, the tinseled sweets
Of news. He blamed dark girls, their tawdry strolls
With greasy Jews toward a carved repose.

IV. Suspect

Nobody ever noticed him at dusk —
Two vacant orbs inhabiting a husk,
His hair dyed black and cufflinks brusquely shined,
One hand raised haltingly as though he signed

To some acquaintance in a red foam booth
Beside the avenue of moll and sleuth,
Or maybe just to draw attention from
Himself toward a uniformed noncom.

So that in retrospect no one could say
What made him stand out from the dying day
Or mark the cut of what he wore or far
Removed, recall a small distinctive scar.

His hands were of the type to sculpt or play
A violin or on an impulse slay,
Well-trained to tease apart or crush with brawn
Whatever pliant thing he practiced on —

His mouth sealed like the cryptic envelope
Sent to the cops, a cipher's pitch and slope
Made plain enough to give away the crime
To anyone with world enough and time.

V. Medford Mass

A granite block on Salem Street beside
The vanished school where once she nodded off
In civics class or smoked behind the gym,
Imagining herself the go-between
Seduced by moonlight and exotic palms
Into eloping with the leading man.

A plaque of burnished bronze sunk into quartz
With buffed New England studs, announcing that
The town of clipper ships and Nassau rum,
White slavers' pens and red brick factories
Now welcomes her reluctantly back home
To rocky soil and Mystic River bends
Who drank the lotus wine of clicking frames
Accelerating into fickle fame.

VI. Taking A Walk With Elizabeth

It is night again, summer of '65, and
I am living at 15 on the streets of Los Angeles.
I don't want to go to school, I don't want
To learn about the great men of history or
The sides of a regular triangle. I only
Want to wait in the Biltmore lobby
For the dishwater blonde cigarette lady
To rub my knee and slip me Newports
From her spaghetti strap handbag.
The doorman knows what's happening
But doesn't care; he lets me sleep sitting up
On the sofa beneath conquistadores
And padres until some sob sister complains
And I stagger off more wasted than when
I crashed and burned, clutching a
Bowler hat and braided suitcase
Like props from the wrong movie —
When suddenly a twilight phantom
Of grease stains and lipstick,
Sawbucks and suede gloves
Collars me with gentle insistence.

And crossing the street into darkness
I feel the breath of a woman
Cold and sour with the sadness
Of an unlived life, and hear her
Slight mincing steps though I see
Nothing but the neon of bodegas
And adult bookstores. And lonely
For company I hang with her
All the way to Washington Boulevard
And the bloody suitcase and the rest
Because she has taken me by the arm
And asked me to be her friend
In the time that is left of our youth
And our dreams. And as we walk
We smell more powerfully than blood
The sea that left us waiting
With our luggage by the pier —
Tomorrow's unborn monsters
Populating lost frontiers.

Exotica

I

"Deliciousness itself..." the verdict of Twain
while Jefferson Davis found it
easier to abstain

(conceding cherimoyas might appeal
to escaped convicts or beggars
in need of a meal).

These trees bore a few offspring deformed
as nuclear artichokes one summer,
green sparks transformed

from dusted pistils to luscious manna
shanghaied between rose petals
and an overripe banana.

I have languid blood, find bracing plums
and sprightly ales less appealing
than sugar cane and island rums.

And when a late summer monsoon
overtops desert peaks
at 4 in the afternoon

I sniff among creosotes
and gaunt prickly pears
the cloying fruit of jungle boats.

II

Between a hennaed nail salon
and taco stand the market
run by a family from Saigon

hosted a stuffed green iguana
contemplating crowded shelves
of exotic flora and fauna.

Near the back a few hedgehogs
from Manila nestled beside black
fuzzy eggs shirtless as Tagalogs,

dark russet to bright orange or tan
and nearly big as jackfruit smuggled
aboard a freighter or rogue sampan —

it took you hours to unthaw a Tutong
in the sideyard beside the basil patch
(even whole it smelled all wrong),

a rusty machete hissing as it
struck the spiny outer shell and
left a dangerous alien split

in half among swooning dandelions.
Nervously we spooned out clots
of chambered gore, like Mayans

straddling sacrificial blocks,
sniffing onions, vanilla beans
and rotting prawns on Mekong docks —

"apples of knowledge" someone laughed
when I stumbled past a garbage can
at dawn, reeling among a daft

swarm of emerald June bugs
swarming the durian shell
like K-9 sniffers lured by drugs

in the luggage of businessmen
(retirees grow oranges
or even mangoes now and then

their double-paned solaria
mocking homeless transplants
like Christmas luminarias).

III
And for no better reason than
the nerve of Sunday daubers
who think they're Paul Gauguin

I spend hours every year
ministering to a yellow sapote
condemned to the wrong hemisphere,

battling sunscald and cutter bees,
soil too alkaline or sodden as clay,
petitioning on arthritic knees

for dripping trophies of latex
sweeter than candied yams
and gamier than sex —

a madman's folly I justify
with Navels and Valencias
that dependably fructify

(an exoticist must make do
sometimes with common fare,
swapping Auvergne Bleu

and Nouveau Beaujolais
for queso and beer
from an end cap display).

Head in the clouds, I dig tunnels
through caliche, flood shallow roots
with liquid compost in runnels

and when bare hedges burn
like cartons of Eskimo Pies
trudge with a kerosene lantern

and grumpy dog in tow,
unleashing orchard heaters'
hissing jack-o-lantern glow

to shelter the fruit of wishes
sown in spring and coaxed
through infernos repetitious —

damned rigid cellulose!
I'll make a chainsaw rev,
bidding last year Adios

at the beginning of May
and brashly setting sail
for the apples of Cathay.

2012—2020

Scout

April is the cruelest month...

500 cans of button mushrooms
and a dead body on the floor
of the 4th floor apartment
overlooking Flatbush Avenue,

5 feet 8 inches, 90 lbs soaking wet
in rumpled sweat pants
and a windbreaker
sprawled atop piles of
hastily scribbled notes

a planet person,
takes a 20 dollar cab fare
to get around him

looks like Tarzan
plays like Jane

big man
fat man
a big dancing bear
with happy feet

if he wants it enough

will the lights come on
by Christmas?

Hiding from Haitians
Senegalese and Puerto Ricans
at the Parade Grounds

calling in their penny ante debts
with shivs or midnight specials

a polite little man with a dog
named Brooks Robinson

his old Jewish mother
a caricature out of Arbus
by way of Alan Sherman
"my son the statistician...."

Fear of letting go, letting up

fear that someday
the numbers wouldn't be enough
or the high school injuries
or test scores whispered into
a tape recorder

and he'd wind up a bum
with nothing to sleep on
but 40s and 3-cone drills
in a freezing apartment,
no degree no girlfriend

just a little dog
licking his hands
glued to a keyboard
and the ghosts of Sal Maglie
and Whitey Lockman.

Because he'd joined no union,
observed no sacred days
inherited no franchise
or guild membership

just 18 hours a day
stitching together a life
moment to moment
from printouts of track meets

blazoned in red dust
and the scraggly pokeweed
of Southern practice fields.

Three VCRs whooshing
wet snow burying
play forts and skateboards

tortured angles of knees
turning radii of hips
elbow positions
reversed and fast forwarded

measurables....

Finally nothing left
but a suspicious dry cough

and the grinning skull
of an anorexic Pope
with a nerd's jagged haircut
and stacks of unread mail.

After all the inconsistencies
falling through the cracks,
the rumors to question
anecdotes to file away

everything
never included in
the final draft report
slipping past
Newton's fantasy

leaving behind
a faded baseball cap
and bent hands
of dry-eyed stopwatches.

2010—2015

Submarine

In Memory of Jim Mulvihill

At the top of my voice,
I sing the praises of
Vassily Alexandrovich Arkhipov
son of Staraya Kupavna
beside the Shalovka River

where the Holy Trinity Church
of gilded onion domes
and crooked footposts
hosts cuckoos and finches.

Home to factories manufacturing
generic pharmaceuticals and
wildfires jumping rivers
of shimmering arsenic

to ordinary merchants who
shrug at legless beggars
hawking Swiss watches

and boys in pushup bras
and black mesh stockings
swapping fixes
beneath cover of nightfall.

As once it gave birth to
the cadet who saved a planet
of atheists and bricklayers
manicurists and morticians

for the Five Year Plan the
Great Society the Trickle Downs
in sunny rose gardens
or Muzak-deadened malls.

As once it despised the lad
of modest ambition
who crawled into a furnace
with a flathead screwdriver

and began to glow
in thirty years
like a nightstand clock.

The same who spoke
like Battel to the Wehrmacht
or Petrov to a few
green dots on a screen
the word NO.

As never the Catholic bishop
to the Gestapo Hauptmann,
as never Generalissimo Eisenhower
to the shareholders
of the United Fruit Company.

As never Roosevelt to Stalin
the CIA to Hussein
talent agents in fancy cars
to Midwestern corn maidens
with opiate eyes —

The refusal to yield
to ordinary madness
or be buttonholed by fear

as the oxygen ran out
and panic blossomed

silently as torpedoes
compressing distance
and time.

Not to secure the peace
of career diplomats
lining halls of banners
and bronze stags

not by means of treaties
or exceptions to
treaties

agreed upon by little men
residing far from their
partitioned buffers and
unincorporated zones.

Not for the clean scribes
or pomaded analysts
the cautiously disguised
sybils and gatekeepers

not even to benefit
the last elephant
shot by ivory poachers
or salmon poaching
in a toxic reservoir.

But because
he wanted to live
another five minutes

to see his son's eyes
sparkle like zircons
after his evening bath

or the knowing look on his
wife's face when she
pretended to be listening
to what he said.

Because anything can happen
in the canyon between
downbeat and decaying cadence

or because he believed
the captain was a vain man
an ambitious man

a man who would follow protocol
even if the clocks stopped
and history baked a shopkeeper's
atoms into the sidewalk.

For any reason good or bad
wise or frivolous
KEPT THE WORLD
FROM CONSUMING ITSELF
IN FIRE.

The one never celebrated
by Moscow Oblast
with a plaque
on the side of a building

Vassily Alexandrovitch Arkhipov

Who didn't hear the ghosts
of cherry trees weep
in a blackened meadow
or armies of cockroaches

skittering among
labyrinths of
canned fruit and
powdered milk

Vassily

Alexandrovitch

Arkhipov

timelessly proclaiming *nyet*
on the bottom of the
Sargasso Sea
serenaded by
loggerhead sharks
and barracudas

arguing with chaos
for one more chance
to shed
the melted
paraffin wings

of superhero or martyr.

Mary Flannery In Hell

Too modest to believe her sufferings
Bought her a seat at Heaven's throne, she shied
From low displays of faith, attempting to
Become more pleasing in the sight of God
By scaring misfits into seizing Grace.

Another decade and the boastful march
Of science would have found a better way
To stiff Salvation's welcome chorus,
Disarming poisons with dialysis
Forgiving multitudes agin' or fer us

While Satan flogged his medicine show
Of sheeted phantoms dragging bottled air
Through annexes of Hell — love's final act
A comedy of chicken broth and Jell-o cubes
Served up by condescending Baptist rubes.

Conquest Of The Ether

What were you doing, Lev Sergeyivich,
When suddenly it came into your head
To build a box of rods and wires that spoke
The eerie language of the floating dead?
Were you about to prime a samovar
And brew the smoky tea that you preferred
With solitaire, or harvest chamomiles
From sylvan glades where bogatyrs had stirred?

The apparatchiks wanted new machines
To track the Five Year Plan's old enemies
To smell revisionists in bolshie streets
Or planted in the bowels of factories.
But you, embracer of the cause, felt more
In love with cleverness than right or wrong,
Less haunted by bourgeois conspiracies
Than four-bar phrases of a peasant song.

To tear the veil of silence without touch
Or summon regiments of tinkling bells
From stillness deep as ruts in woodland snow
And all without bewitching orchestras
Of catgut, lacquered wood and valves aglow —

It kept your mind awake at night! When Lenin
Showed he had the knack, you stepped aside
And watched him pull a bluebird from the air
While deputies and commissars gaped wide
As children at the Sorochinsky fair.

Of nothingness we learn it's full of waves
That ebb and flow and overtop the crests
Of bosoms slight and forearms choked by pearls,
Presenting to the ear and mind a trace
Of who approaches, standing still, and who
Retreats while never stirring from their place.

Seductive absence dwells in everything,
Its fluctuating fields the basis of
Our loneliness and joys — while gross attempts
To conquer that elusive no man's land
May sound unbeautiful as banshee gliss
Torn from the ether by a clumsy hand.

(In later years Lev Termen spent his days
Designing toys the KGB concealed
In consulates of silent men whose crimes
Played dumb behind an Eagle's wooden shield —

Still consumed by the flirt of nothingness
Inhabiting rouged cheeks and beauty moles,
He draped her bones in disembodied thoughts
While plying flesh with sparkling wines and soles.)

Identity

People try to lasso
  the wind
with empty chairs.
  Like they did
with the boy named
  marius who was
the brother of
  denis, who died
in the afternoon
  after being kicked
by a goat and soon
  gave his name
to marius just to
  stay alive until

another brother,
  phoebus, departed
during a contest
  with an oboe player.
And saw his name
  passed on to the
boy who thought
  he was marius
until becoming denis
  after the change was
recorded in the parish
  register so phoebus

would live on in the
  ill-fitting disguise
of a changeling brother.
  Then maria died
and they changed

the name of
marius/denis/phoebus,
this time to maria
who'd sometimes wanted
to draw angels
in the snow with
golden darts
or kill a rabbit
with a slingshot.

And she who'd also
tried to hide
her voice behind an
agreeable smile
learned to love the
hot winds caressing
a pair of stork's
ungainly legs
in summer or winter's
rough tongue
nuzzling cobblestones
and bare twigs

even as death kept
harvesting the
shiny apples of
untended orchards.
Growing by losses
into the only
villager who could
claim nobody
and everyone.

Low Average Does Not Qualify For Assistance

They kept changing the name
from borderline to slow
to unspecified LD.

But they couldn't speed up
the ice age
of cursive drills
and multiplication
tables.

The autistics and
neurodivergents
weave in and out
of crumbling lanes

but I am stuck
in low gear
on a straightaway

where it's always
twilight in winter
and Barstow
turns into Amboy.

I want to trade
my empty pride
for a guilt check
at the beginning
of every month.

But there are
too many others
born in the
25th percentile

competing for a
box of potato buds
and a pee-stained
mattress.

1986

Sacred Space

If you shut
your eyes tight
God is who
you see

when you know
exactly where
your nose
is going to be.

The devil's when
you touch it
and feel the sin
of pride

aiming for
the darkness
and never
landing wide.

Little Myth

He dreamed how someday
he'd be semi-autonomous
the first riverhorse
not just hippeponymous.

Pandora's Inbox

I tried to feed a starving child
Who stared at me accusingly
Through swollen orbs of fevered eyes
Bribing death to set them free.

But from that well-intended thought
A sea of monsters swarmed to life
And choked my e-mail server caught
Between incoming waves of strife:

Doomed polar bears atop their shelf
Of ice consumed by warming days
Or elephants gunned down for pelf
To line the walls of proud chalets

A lab rat tortured to appease
The itch for creams and vitamins
That boost superfluous hormones
Or suction years from double chins.

I saw each isolated cost
But not entangled webs of horror:
The more I tried to shut the box
The wider yawned a buried door.

Cyber Bully

Afterwards the neighbors
always say

he never stood out
in an obvious way,

played clarinet in
the marching band

volunteered at a
lemonade stand.

Why act surprised?
A book's thin covers

conceal dark thoughts
and darker lovers

when out of the blue
lightning strikes

torching frameups
of likes and dislikes.

Deep State

the sound of tacit
agreements

multiplying
in secret bunkers:

a few old monkeys
pensively scratching
their balls

black potatoes
sprouting eyes
on a crowded bus
in July

Monuments

There is a big pile of shoes
underneath my desk
and they are a family
with no address.

Where were they all headed
when the alarm bell sounded
and what happened to their feet
falling upwards into winter?
.
The shoes are too close
sunlight can't penetrate
the fugues of their armor.

Sunlight is retreating
to the hush of beaten wings

to fossil toads of proclamations
and boxes of broken swords
multiplying in attics.

This is anybody's day to own.
The shoes won't stop you.

Dependency

I heard if you
stopped fighting
the mud embrace
of the whirlpool

it would let go of
your dinosaur
bones.

I decided to
try it

before the sun set
and rose again
over the earth's
crumbling mask.

But the sweet chimes
of thirst

only tricked me deeper
into a dead mother's
protective arms

and smoothed
jagged splinters
of unhealed
exit wounds

with milk mirages
of lifeless sand.

Proofreading

Downtown isn't the same
without the barrel of
lead slugs squeezed
between a laundromat
and flower shop.

Where is the bandaged vet
who directed traffic
with rolled-up editorials,
his shaved black skull
shiny as napalm?

Where are the old typesetters
from Philly or Jersey City
who knew all the mysteries
of Garamond
Palatino and Centaur,

remembered which fonts
wanted to be gapped
snugger than the points
on an old Ford

and the difference
between horsey
and bold?

Where's the day-shift
proofreader
with the green visor
and dry-cleaned smile

(who could spot
italicized periods
and broken
6 point type)?

Suspicious of
new-fangled tubes
and circuit boards

he gave up
his union benefits
and two-week vacations

and finally his livelihood
to the smartly-kerned
display types
in leather pumps
and pushup bras

straggling from
the business college
down the street.

Nobody cared that I
dropped out of
high school
and earned
a GED

only that I showed up
to the graveyard shift
on time

sleepwalking through
columns of numbers
and words I didn't
understand

back in the days before
knowledge grew obsolete
one missing pair of eyes
at a time.

1990

Brick And Mortal

The lights were too bright
and everybody talked too fast
and looked at me
like I didn't belong.

Sometimes a NASCAR
mama with freckled arms
dropped a ten-spot
and change on the counter

gawking in amazement
when I tried to add the
numbers in my head
and kept getting lost.

Then just to be mean
she'd ask me for change
and toss a few more
green logs on the fire

(after I thought
we were done)

until the manager
had to step in and
zero out the sale
with simmering eyebrows
and a glued-on smile.

After the third night
they told me not to
come back.

But that's how it goes
when you're too old
to stack pallets
in July

or move shiny sofas
on four bald tires

but you still need to work
the dead end job
you've been doing
your whole life —

trying to remember
where a chit goes
or a gift card
embossed with
cartoon Santas.

Still worried about
peeing in your
pants or tasting battery
acid when you mess up
on a test.

Still scared to tell
the doctor
the school nurse
or your mama

how you feel an
electric current
shooting up and down
your backbone

and sliding between
your legs
like a feather
through mud

every time failure
bounces you
rough as an uncle
with beer on his breath

and a coppery cold
glint in his eye.

Bad Dog

Because he didn't have
the woman anymore

or part-time job
he'd overslept
once too often
for the manager
to ignore

(just afternoons
of buzzing idleness
in a hammock of
inner tubes
strung between
station breaks)

he thought of plugging
everyone on the
afternoon shift
when they left
with their paychecks

(managers in cotton knits
and shiny receptionists
falling like acorns
in a hailstorm).

But because he was
too chicken
went instead
to a lawn sale

and got in trade for
a hydraulic jack
and cordless lava lamp

a big brown dog with
ears like corn husks
and a tongue that
hung sideways

from his battle-scarred
muzzle and flews
like a battered
turnip chute.

And taught that dog
how to aim for the nuts
and ask questions later

sicking him on a
gunny sack baited with
venison scent

or sprinkling chiltepins
and black powder
into his kibble.

But when they told him
to get the dog fixed
so he wouldn't
chase cats and
mail carriers

he turned
six shades of green

remembering the yearlings
on his uncle's ranch,

their bawling pleas
and terror-swollen eyes
and buckets of calf fries
glistening in the sun.

Don't preach
he growled
carrying the dog
to the vet's back room

after a scrap with a
neighbor's
brindle feis.

And they'd tell him again
why he needed
to let them cut the
bruised agates
of wanderlust

from the tight
velveteen pouch
beneath the dog's tail

and spoke of laws
and regulations
fines and court
appearances.

But hearing them
repeat themselves

only reminded him of
factory whistles
cold coffee and managers
polishing reputations

and how he'd screwed
himself coming and going
to feed scraps of paper
to a hole in the earth
where nothing lived.

And after they were
done talking
he reminded them
once more

how he'd never let
his dog grow fat
in the shadow of an
outlived dream

like some roustabout
washed up cowboy
living on the dole.

Because what is a man
or a dog when he
can't chase
the prophet of his hunger

past the leash laws
of lawyers and
politicians?

One afternoon
he heard a squeal of tires
and the sigh of
empty flour sacks
rifled by the wind

and knew without looking
that his dog had
disappeared into
the final calamity

of spinning axles
and smoking brakes.

And after burying
what was left
in an army blanket,

a startled bloody grin
fixed to his brain
like Jesus' eyes
on his grandmother's
calendar

he went back to the trailer
drank a beer
and nodded along with
the listeners on the radio

scared of all the strays
that needed to be
fixed.

Minor Character (from the movie "Our Vines Have Tender Grapes")

Waking before sunrise
Ingeborg saw colors
from another planet
inside the secret room
where her father laid his head.

Ingeborg Jensen, 17,
a man's strong hands
for picking potatoes
or mending harnesses

two tender grapes
crowning a twisted vine
for stained hands
to pluck.

Classified as feeble-minded
by the doctor from Kenosha
wearing a butcher's smock
and smoking a cheap cigar

before the town threw her a parade
with black Packards hay wagons
and Bible verses
brittle as cornrows.

Telling her story
would have meant
everything wasn't
just noble farmers
and greedy capitalists

the uninsured barn
and child's sacrifice
accompanied by
swelling violins.

And Ingeborg more than
just a girl who got married
had a baby and died
all on the same day

trying to find a path
to the river
where her mother
laid her head.

Oh Be A Fine Girl, Kiss Me

(Annie Jump Cannon)

She didn't have the type of face
To launch a fleet of battleships
Or make the local lads give chase
To icy spheroids of her hips.

Nor did she covet gilded things
Included with a wedding day:
A mansion's well-appointed wings
And lawns for tennis or croquet.

But shared a yen with Amherst waif
For shadow-draped immensities
Of austere rooms immune to grief
And passionate intensities

Where old explosions left behind
Dark interstellar traffic jams
And jostling threads of spectral lines
More wondrous than scorpions or rams.

Displaying airy ravishments
Surpassing any earthbound jewel,
The next unplanned near-accident
Obedient unto her rule.

The Second Fire

Engulfed by flames one distant winter night,
The tabernacle's buttressed walls still loom
For doves and starlings floating in the light
Of gutted chancery and choir room.

The gleaming offices next door won't sneer
At how dry rot invades a rector's floor
Or portion out a calculated tear
For worshippers turned from the padlocked door

But thrust their labyrinths of sterile suites
Towards the muffled God who dwells apart
From shuttered coffee shops and idle streets,
Official pity frozen in His heart.

Beneath a vanished gargoyle's pointed chin
A faithful prostitute observes the glow
Announcing conflagration set within
By homeless residents of squatter's row

Defying regulations and the fuzz
Patrolling Caesar's loaves and fish —
Who, after quaffing sweet communion buzz,
Snore praise more genuine than tithing's dish.

1972

Any Election

I.
The Big Night

The sandwiches and cupcakes brace against
Limp slabs of Brie and skewered chunks of ham
While party goers with their shoulders tensed
Cringe at the latest test for Uncle Sam.
What does it mean, this slow unraveling
Too unbelievable for shock or tears?
And how'd we botch the omens of the spring
While mocking prophets' righteous fears?

But as suspense yields way to awkward fact
I won't embrace the easy course of blame.
This night will yield to dawn and I must act
Against deceitful cynics' parlor game
By realizing inner commonwealths
Of thought and action, seed and bundled grain.

II.
The Passage of Time

It's been three years since charlatan-elect
Swore on the Holy Book he desecrates
To guard, preserve and lawfully protect
The Constitution of these fractured States.
He grows more nervous by the hour and speaks,
As those before him, in confusing words
Which yet betray his lingering disdain
For motley caravans of unmasked herds.

While shrugged aside by partisans' shrill noise
One truth still lingers like a mythic plebiscite
Unclaimed — to plainly speak the awful choice
The angriest must make between the rights
Of beasts in jungles and a tiny voice
Ignored by talking heads and viral parasites.

2016—2020

Incongruity

Love handles poke
From a tilted rump,
Left leg askew
From how I slump

To fit dimensions
Where medians dwell,
Content to inhabit
An agreeable hell

Of overhead lamps
Claustrophobically looming
And Procrustean car seats
Adjustably zooming.

"Don't bend," they preached,
"Be proud of your height,"
The summer I rose
In glandular flight

Above those destined
By cheekbones to wed
The sons and daughters
Of privilege inbred.

The last one chosen
I scrambled at third
Until sentenced to right
By the high scoring herd

So I wouldn't permit
The go-ahead run,
Coming up empty
Or jumping the gun —

A package arriving
With no guarantees
Hard on the heels
Of night fantasies

When shadows fled
The tale of the tape,
Exposing a whopper
Hung like a grape.

1973

North Of Flagstaff

How much precious silence remained for them
To kill, how cold the bitterroot clump of
Ash on the morning they broke drover's camp,
Two waddies in chaps and hand-me down
Work shirts, a Georgia shavetail and a
Bucktoothed Apache rising up slowly
From burnt scraggly beards of buffalograss
And the unclaimed land of shared mistrust.

How cautiously, deliberately they
Hitched the trailer, drove on in silence
With lead pieces tucked to their sides,
How the stars shone and the world's peace rose
As they sailed toward pie and coffee,
The good of all loss gone into gentle guns.

Crossword Cheat

Do I believe they're more than just a way
To hide from doing other urgent jobs
Like stringing cylinders of chicken wire
Around a few bedraggled pepper shrubs
Or pulling weeds from bird-grimed paver stones?
No matter, when a hallway's meager span
Suffices for my inattentive mind
To misplace wallet, keys or soda can
It's time again to snatch the puzzle page
From hefty garbage bags of grapefruit rinds
And runny aftermaths of breakfast eggs.

The mind more rigid than arthritic knees
And not lured by an intersecting track
Defying customary straightaways
Is destined for the airless cul-de-sac
Of protein shakes and TV comedies
Attendant on remote. So I'll ride *gnu*
Attired in *obi* trying like hell to mend
Criss-crossing wires of mislaid memories
While sneaking nervous glances at The End.

2018—2020

The Yearning I

I am walking down the long pink hall
I am walking down the long orange hall
I am looking for my beautiful boyfriend
I am looking for my beautiful girlfriend
They have given me a map to the sun porch
They have given me a map to the brown lawn
I hear the music behind the third door
I hear the music behind the fourth door
There is no joy or sadness in the music
There are no trees or oceans in the music
I have never seen my boyfriend's face
I have never seen my girlfriend's face
They are too far away from the earth
They are too far away from the stars

The Yearning II

Sometimes when I
can't sleep
and keep staring
at the clock
on the hi-fi speaker

a stranger with candy
in his eyes
asks me

to come outside
where the hay is sweet
and summer days
are long.

And I want to do it
but I'm scared
to fly

and my yearning
is a symphony
of dark faces

ruled by a
conductorless
baton.

The Yearning III

I remember a
boy in a bus station
who locked eyes
with me
and wouldn't look down

and a woman
seated at a bar

who squeezed my hand
tighter and tighter
and wouldn't let go.

I will never know
what they meant

fear, hopelessness,
wonder
defiance

but for a little while
I felt a string
tying us together

and it weighed less
than a single blade
of grass.

Pornography

Stuck in the elevator
on the 13th floor

no way
up or down

the only
other passenger

a used catalogue
of spare parts.

From somewhere
a voice
offers a way
out

if I stop
pushing on
the emergency
button.

And suddenly I feel
the elevator shaft
between my legs

a cool weightlessness
of lines never drawn
on a skin
that can't hide.

In Praise Of Small Talk

The well-adjusted like to
gossip about tv stars
and trade lo carb diets
at the doctor's office.

Once upon a time
I thought I was better,
digging for jars of
ancient honey
in forbidden tombs.

Now I wonder if maybe
the witnesses to Dachau
or Jonestown

babbled about baseball
or what they had
for dinner last night?

(fearful of the silence
where witches hung
like poisoned apples).

Maybe what fell
like ordinary rain
was the sound of
children

dwarfed by
trees of statistics
and ashes baked into
footnotes

trying to sing
their way home.

Loss Of Memory

The doctor said
it was
sometimes
hard to tell

being born
a little
slow

from dragging out
the last
farewell.

So make ready my tires
for an unbalanced load
and patches of fog
beside a slick road.

A Self-Help Guru In Assisted Living

He had a scientific mind, but not
A strict consistent one. That is to say
He'd love an elegant hypothesis
Supported by the facts and equally
The wordless arguments of silky legs,
Encircling Delius with peptide chains
While breakfasting on nova lox and eggs.

When Ms. So-and-so invited him
To lecture on the Narrow Path, he said
Go show your backside to a mirror, bend down
And blow a playful kiss at God. At ninety-one
He finds milkshakes and burgers beat dried kelp,
Plays footsie with the giggling volunteer
Who likes his wolf goatee and randy yelp.

Love Your Disease

but don’t let her think
you need her
in order to live
like a renter

inside your own
skin.

Keep her guessing
like she kept you
waiting at the bar

packed and ready
for the organ recital
and carnations in
cellophane.

But don’t forget
to call her
on the anniversary
of your first date

because you don’t
want her to think
there’s somebody else

sharing the little cafe
with the drab green
awning

where you
wobble around
a blind axis
keeping your
uneasy distance.

So many ways to
dance alone, so many
plans to execute a chasse
or kick

concentrating
on the tightness
of line and

precision of angle.

Until suddenly
she's close enough
to whisper
in your ear

and ask if
you want to go
somewhere
else

maybe even
the back seat
of the long black limo

where dancing's
easy as butter.

Seborrhea

Where do they
come from these

pale schools
of blind fish
shrinking from the sun?

I thought people
were more like rivers
than crystal rock
mirages

so why is there never
an end to this

hard accumulation
of sticky
crumbles

vanished dreams
unfinished
projects?

To rancid bricks
peeling away
like post-it notes

from bodies
shed and consumed
over the lifetime
of the bearer.

Man With A Smartphone

See the man
see his mouth move
back and forth.

He needs to
disconnect from
the bloodless ether

he needs to tip
the sax man
blowing hymns
in the parking lot

just for Jesus
just for the earth
hot and new
beneath his feet.

The birds tell me this
the space rocks tell me this

the compass fish
of desert seas
whisper it
in my sleep.

Jealousy

The clouds persist

and sometimes a
limp orange blob
collapses into
a tightening
spin.

Everyone has a
stationary low
in the summer

when the green eye
of sleeplessness.
hovers
above a deserted
village —

bleeding through
muddy window panes

chasing a suspicious
ball of yarn
down feline curves
of spiral steps.

Two Days Before The Hurricane

The jersey cows have to
ride out the storm
because there's no time
to truck them to safety

and no higher ground
but the ruined porches
of rumors.

They have been here
before.

They will turn their backs
against the wind
and lower their heads
into a circle
of white flames.

Some will wake up
surprised on their
own tiny islands

after the soft knock
of sunrise.

And some will bawl
dark as bruises
and cold as milk
on steel.

Old Age

The wind's stiff fur
rubs up against me.

Sometimes like a puppy
it licks my face

sometimes it leaves a present
in the middle of the sidewalk.

Nobody hears it tipping
overflowing barrels

of forgotten addresses
and blank commands.

Meanwhile every evening
a few stars come out

the wind dies down a
dog has chased his tail

to the edge of sleep.

2021

Inheritance

Folded green wings
fragile as
silk ribbons

lead a blind horse
through a
ruined choir.

A jailer's rope
slithers off
and falls asleep.

Father,
show me
where I join
the sea.